Supersession
and other writings
by Hannah Toney

ISBN: 978-1-312-33677-3

Copyright 2014 © Hannah Toney

Any reproduction of this work, or parts of this work, outside of a review, is prohibited without exclusive permission from the author. All rights reserved.

A Note from Hannah

This book is a re-release of my very first chapbook. I took some things out and added some things in, but overall, it is still Supersession. *I first put together* Supersession *at Governor's School for the Arts in the summer of 2013, to showcase what I had learned and created while I was there. The majority of the content remains the same, with a few things removed to be saved for future publications, and some new additions for length. The biggest change is the addition of my short story,* Multi-Hit Wonder, *as the penultimate piece. I hope you all enjoy!*

As for dedications, it is still dedicated to my parents, Richard and Beth Toney, my "parents" Sarah Lin McInteer and Danny Washing, my good friends, Jonah Chili Brooks and Catherine Matar, as well to my fellow-squirrel watcher, Erica Roe, and the love of my life, Daniel Simpson (don't worry, I wrote everything in here before I met you; none of the angtsy love poems were inspired by you!). I will again give acknowledgment to my greatest influences, Chuck Palahniuk, Bret Easton Ellis, Vladimir Nabokov, e. e. cummings, Barabara Gowdy, and Ian McEwan.

Table of Contents

December 3rd

Sarah and Danny

Preview

Miracle

and then he was

Coping

Kentucky

Damaged

Discouragement

Denial

Mild Irritations

sometimes i look

Wishes

Miss' Game

Just Like You

Romance vs Practicality

A Personal Essay in November

untitled

All Made Up

my day with jacob

Matthew Donovan

SMS

Playing Favorites

Elude

Have You Again

Can't Keep Away

Multi-Hit Wonder

Supersession

December 3rd

December 3rd, 2012

Ultimate happiness

One confession

All I ever wanted

Burned out

December 28th, 2012

Beginning of the end

The end lasts an eternity

Struggle, collapse

No hope, never

January, February

March, April

It's over now, over

Yet my thoughts dwell

Permanently reside on

December 3rd, 2012

Sarah and Danny

Kindness

Sarah Lin Elizabeth McInteer

Daniel Scott Washing

Sarah and Danny

Danny, my first sincere friend

Sarah, my greatest encouragement

The first two to show me

The idea of friendship

Is not a myth

Treating me like a person

Making me feel real

Showed me kindness

Saved me

Preview

This is a preview of what's to come

Don't you dare cast down your eyes

You knew what you were getting into

You can't say I didn't warn you

Yet you still claim to "love" me

I wonder if it's so conditional now

And this is only the beginning

The main attraction goes steeply downhill

So you better make eye contact

Bite your lip and shut the hell up

Because this was all your choice

You can't blame me for your stupidity

And I really did try to warn you, my dear

So now that our little preview is done

Dry those tears and get ready

It only gets worse from here

Miracle

I wake up to the miracle of that caramel skin. I wake up to the miracle of those springy, dark curls, the full lips, the piercing, dark eyes. The smooth baritone, bidding me good morning as he turns to the girl on the other side of him, paying her more attention just to see my reaction.

I wake up to the miracle of another day as a dutiful slave, never complaining. I wake up to the miracle of being kept around, even though he has her now. To the name-calling and insults and the occasional sweet remark followed by a laugh because I actually fell for it.

I wake up to the miracle of you.

and then he was

"It just might be you," the man says to the boy and the boy has never been quite right but he wants it to be him so he lets it go and he hides and he grows and he gets so close and then.

Well. Then, he falters. The face cracks, but it is him, and he is a man now too, and he overshadows the man who once showed him what he wanted to become and he is there, he is there.

But he falters and he cries for help, and the man says, "It was never you," and then he is a boy again and then. Nothing.

Coping

They meet each other there one night, neither one expecting the other. She, for the name on the stone was her lover, meant the world to her. He, for the name on the stone was his close friend, deserving the utmost respect.

They are both silent for a long time, but a conversation starts when he finally speaks up. "He was a great man, wasn't he?"

She's slightly choked up as she nods, and doesn't speak because she's afraid her voice might crack. That's all that's said that night, and there's silence the next few times they see each other there.

One night, though, she feels she's ready to talk, and they do. He's been around longer, he's had more losses, and he knows just how crippling grief can be. That's why he didn't try and get her to talk about it anymore until she was ready, and that's why he'll listen to her now that she is.

And through this, the unlikely pair become friends and see quite a bit of each other. Coping isn't easy at all, but he makes it just a little bit more bearable for her and their bond grows stronger than what either would have thought. She begins to smile again, and he knows he'll keep smiling, at least for her sake.

If only she had known that the next time she'd see there, it would be his name and not his face.

Kentucky

They say the state tree is a dogwood, but I rarely ever see any

I see cardinals a lot but I don't understand why it's the mascot for the University of Louisville, rather than the University of Kentucky

God, I want to go to U of L, but my mom hates the idea of me leaving Lexington

I often say anything would be better than Lexington, but then I realize I'm forgetting about Winchester and don't even ask me about anything not directly around Lexington

Speaking of mascots, what's up with the Wildcat? Is it the same as a bob cat? Is the bob cat even the state animal?

I really, really hate Kentucky and the only reason I want to go to Louisville is to adjust a bit to bigger city life

I'm going to upsize a bit until I finally get the hell out of her and make my escape to Chicago or Los Angeles or another stereotypical big city

Anywhere as long as it isn't Danville or Harrodsburg or Nicholasville or Versailles or Winchester or Richmond or Mount Sterling or Georgetown or Frankfort or itty bitty Burgin

And I sure as fuck don't want to stay in Lexington

It often surprises me how big this sad state is, with so many places I've never visited or maybe even heard of

Paducah is a mystery to me and what exactly is a Kenton county?

By the way, I think the state flower is the goldenrod and I don't know how many counties or cities there are but you can ask my mamaw; she knows everything

She's my polar opposite in terms of all things Kentucky and where I'm repulsed, she's fascinated

She used to lecture and quiz me as a child and that's why I know the colors are blue and gold and that the first governor was Isaac Shelby

So many Kentucky writers have pride, but I fall into the "I hate my home" stereotype and I'm perfectly okay with that

Kentucky's full of horses and basketball and chicken, and though all I eat is chicken and basketball is the only sport that doesn't bore me, I hate it here and I don't belong

Kentucky sucks ass and I'm leaving as soon as I can

Damaged

I am such a clueless idiot

I mean, it's no wonder I always

End up in pain

And it's no wonder I've started to give up

After all, what's the use?

My affection and devotion have never

Done me any good

They have blinded me then turned around

And destroyed me

So why do I even still have faith

Perhaps it's because I'm so damaged

I've stopped caring

Just how bad it hurts

As long as I feel good for a bit

The thrill before the crash

Keeps me coming back for more

Discouragement

I don't want people to know

Because I don't want their discouragement

    As if I didn't already know I'd never have you!

I'm not stupid

I'm not clueless

    You're wonderful, I'm not

After all, I've been here before

And it's a dance I prefer to dance alone

    This passion will burn out, I'm sure

No matter how out-there I am

There are matters in which I am well educated

    Even I know what reality is

So I wish people would stop trying to find out

And once they know, stop discouraging

    Stop warning me, I already know!

i will never be good enough

Denial

As long as you continue to make me smile

I suppose I'll still love you

I'll keep living in this denial

As if you never left me

As if you don't hate me now

As if I have the slightest chance of

Having you again

You see, everything you do

Has the power to earn that smile

And I will ignore the facts

Denial is sweet if I can pretend

That you are still mine

Mild Irritations

I want to believe I hurt you

At least that would mean you cared

Instead, there is no pain, but rather

A mild irritation, that's it

That's all I am to you

And that's all I will ever be

sometimes i look

Sometimes when I look at you

I look just a little bit too long

And sometimes you notice, I think

And sometimes you might acknowledge

But I don't know for sure

I have to make sure I look away quick enough

We don't ever speak but I get the feeling

That you really don't like me at all

It's irrational, yes, but still

There's just something that makes me think

You notice me looking and

You really hate me for that

Should I apologize for these wrongs?

I do not want my eyes always on you

And I really don't want these thoughts

These thoughts I pretend are romantic

Just to distract from what they really are

I don't want to feel drawn to follow

I don't want ever look again

Because sometimes when I look at you

I look for much too long and

I don't think I can ever stop

Wishes

Wishes, wishes, *wishes*

I'll wish again and again

Because those wishes, that wish

    Will never come true

Is all I could ever want

And so I take a breath

Stare at the clock

Whisper what I want

It doesn't come true

    Because wishing is foolish

If you don't say it out loud

There is nothing I've wanted more

And I will keep wishing until

    I learn to face reality

I get what I want most

Miss' Game

"Forgive me, forgive me, forgive me"

She chants, monotone

Blank faced, bang after bang

Screams to God, thud after thud

"Amen," she whispers

Final bang, final thud

Then the cold sterile room

Miss with the wicked grin

Caress or kiss or prod

Pause and giggle

"Well, hello, Father"

She croons, tugs collar

Embalmed, dressed in familiar uniform

Miss prefers him that way

Begins her game, smirks

"Oh, what's this?" Surprise

And a snicker, "Someone, it seems,

Has already had this fun."

Miss always knows when her game has been played without her

Just Like You

I should have forgotten you by now

But can I ever truly forget you?

Whenever anything goes wrong

I find myself remembering you

It makes me sick, the way I let you hurt me

Destroy me, devour me, ruin me

All the while, with your concerns and apologies

All the while, trying to pretend to care

And, like an idiot, I fell for it

Every single time, I fell for it

And every single time, I broke a little more

Now, I'm beyond recognition

And only one thing is clear to all:

Now, I am the one breaking others

Now, I am just like you

Romance vs. Practicality

What would someone like me have to gain from love?

I have no interest in marriage

I dream of any sort of success obtained alone

I am a studious history dork or aspiring fashion icon

But my romantic side won't leave me be

My romantic side wants to write poetry

And my romantic side seems to have fallen in love

He is a repulsive young man

As annoying as he is unbelievably good looking

Rude, arrogant, obnoxious, a stereotypical jerk

And my opposite in so many ways

We'd kill each other in our frequent "moral" debates

And he's far more open (and *loud*) than I

Whenever he speaks, I have to resist the urge

To tell him to just *shut up* already, sit down

He's everything I despise, but unfortunately

My romantic side doesn't see I have no need for love

My romantic side doesn't see he's positively horrible

My romantic side would let him win every argument

My romantic side adores his stupid little outbursts

My romantic side loves him as much as my practical side despises him

A Personal Essay in November

I realize now that you will absolutely never love me and I hate you so much for that. I mean, I still love you, but I really fucking hate you because what is so wrong with me that you don't feel anything? Don't think I didn't notice the correlation between you saying you weren't feeling very sexual and the sudden snappiness and rudeness you've been treating me with. All I asked was for you to plan a date for me, and you flipped shit, like I was asking you to do some big thing. You said you aren't capable of doing something romantic for me. Well, why not? You claim to be some big romantic, but yet you can't do something romantic? Let's face facts: you're about as romantic as a brick, but even a brick would understand that when someone cares about someone else as much I care about you, *anything* would be more romantic than the nothing you're giving me right now. I really don't think you care about me at all. You only want me for sexual purposes, and I'm just kidding myself by acting like we're a real couple. You don't care about me at all, do you? If I had any self-respect, I would break up with you, but I don't want to be alone again and I really do love you so much that I'll continue with the delusion that I could actually make this failure of a relationship better. Baby, we are *so* doomed. But please, please, *please* don't let us be doomed. I want to be with you more than anything else in the whole entire world and I can't lose you now. I just don't understand why you still, after all this time, don't care about me at all. Perhaps I'll make you feel bad, *guilt* you into loving me. It is a low, horrid tactic, but I am desperate and I want you to love me so very badly. Tomorrow, when you come over, I will surprise you with things I know you love and you will have no choice but to contemplate caring for me more than you do now. I will make a list and I will pull all the stops out. Nothing, and I mean *nothing* will stop me from proving that I am the perfect girl for you. God, I am so pathetic. I deserve to die, being so evil and manipulative, but I want to keep you because you are my Last Good Thing and I cannot bear to be alone again. Then I really will have nothing left to live for and even though I despise life as much as I do I cannot stop fighting for something to live for. Oh, if someone would just kill me now, then I would not have to worry ever again. If only I had the guts to do it myself right now, but I don't and I will continue to fight for you. You who will never love me, you who think me ridiculous for thinking that after all this time you would be capable of doing something to make me happy. Why is it so wrong for me to expect you to be my boyfriend for once? Isn't that what you say you are? So tell me why I'm not allowed to treat you like one? You are not my fuck buddy. I love you, but if you don't understand how relationships really work, then I'm only hurting myself by staying with you. I don't want to break up with you, but I don't want to spend forever in this pain and never do anything about it. I want you to love me and I want you to act like you love me. So excuse me for not thinking it's that much of a big deal for me to ask for a date for Christmas.

Untitled

but i don't want to think of this any other way, i don't want to let go of this. who holds the key to my freedom? it could be you but it is most likely me because secretly i do not wish to be. agonizing and burning, let's catch a glimpse before time is up. you are quick; i want to be quicker. what could you possibly see? i want to catch a glimpse of you and catch your eye but it's hard to catch anything. what is it you think and why am i surprised when you don't remember? it should not hurt, it should not hurt. and i try to draw you but i will never get your features right and that little photo does not do you justice because you can't see the shape of your jaw or how a different angle makes your face look entirely different or how sweet your lips are or your real smile, that subtle little curve, and how on certain morning i could squint and see a completely new face that is just as beautiful. i know that when we are apart i will be cured, but i'd rather wallow in this curse than let go.

All Made Up

There's nothing quite like putting makeup on the man of your dreams. No, wait, bear with me for a second, let me explain.

It's totally normal, I swear. We're backstage, it's opening night for our production of *The Wizard of Oz*, the makeup artist is busy painting the Wicked Witch green, he and I are just in the ensemble, and he's my best friend. Not to mention, if anyone knows how to cake on makeup, it's me.

And as for the whole "man of my dreams" thing, I only discovered that recently. He has no idea, and, with any luck, he'll never know. Like I said, he's my best friend, and that's how we'll stay. Never mind how adorable and funny he is, never mind how nicely he dresses or smells, never mind his artistic ability, never mind the fact that he's nicer to me than anyone I've ever met.

First, foundation. Yesterday, he was upset that the color he used made him look ghostly pale, so today I pick a shade that will make him ever-so-slightly more tan than usual. As I begin to smear it on his face and blend, it hits me that this is the closest I'll ever get to caressing him. Oh, don't give me that look, I'd hardly consider that a very creepy remark.

"Am I super pale again?" he asks. Even if he looks in a mirror, he won't be able to tell, because he doesn't have his glasses.

"No, you look really nice," I say, as I put the foundation away and pull out the eyeliner.

"Oh! Why, thank you," he says, almost surprised, and I feel myself blush.

Now comes the hard part of the whole experience. You might have wondered why, if he didn't have his glasses, why he didn't have contacts in. The answer to that question is he may be the most spastic blinker I've ever met in my life.

As usual, I'm unable to keep his eyes open long enough to get more than a small speck of black on him, and I contemplate just leaving it at that, as I did yesterday. But, no, I'm determined, and I keep drawing, even when his eyes close.

When I'm done, the lines are a bit lower than they should be, but they're dark enough and they're there, so I'm satisfied. Blush is a breeze in comparison (and in general), and when I'm done, I move on to lipstick. Oh, to know that something touching his lips will soon touch mine...

Okay, I admit, that's rather creepy. Give me a break, I really can't help it! His lips are just so pleasantly full, and when I dab at the red with my fingers, I feel how soft they are. If I really wanted to, I could lean forward and kiss him...

"Hey! You done with him?" I'm yanked out of my thoughts by our other friend, who is playing the Wizard. Somehow, I ended up responsible for his makeup as well.

"Yeah." I'll repeat the process with him, smearing foundation, struggling (though not quite as much) to draw on eyeliner, dusting his cheeks with blush, and carefully blending in lipstick on lips just as full, but it won't be the same.

There really is nothing putting makeup on the man of your dreams.

If She Knew

She likes me

She is only eleven and she

Has the cutest, most innocent crush

On me

A monster

Oh, if only she knew

If only she knew she would

Run far away

And if only I could

Look away, not care

About the things I care about

If only I could be

Somebody else

Anybody else

Normal, not me

But I want her and

Though I would never touch her

Knowing she thinks

The world of me is

Unbearable and it

Kills me to see her eyes

Light up when I enter the room

If only she knew

If only she'd run

If only I could trust myself

Not to chase after if she did

my day with jacob

Today we spoke but I am not sure if it meant anything because it usually doesn't and you probably won't remember me.

Today I got the chance to be near you but I don't think it counts because how could it?

Today I almost hinted that I liked you but I thought better of it because it really is a good thing that you don't know.

Today I thought of how funny it is that we regard you as an authority figure and, to some, a surrogate father, but in the real world you are young enough that my feelings would not be considered strange.

Today I joked with you and it made me think that maybe we might be close to acquaintances now and it's okay for me to smile when we cross paths, but you might forget me again and that would be uncomfortable.

Today I thought about you nearly constantly and let slip to a few people that I like you, but I'm still afraid to join in a crush gossip section because what if it isn't normal for me to like you?

Today I got a good view of your lips and decided that I would really like to kiss you but of course I won't and I don't need to explain why.

Today I got to study your build and noticed that your stomach sticks out just a little bit and I really like that about you, though I've never been able to explain why I hate muscles so much.

Today I wrote poetry about you but I was vague enough that I don't think anyone could figure out it was you because I don't know who will be reading those poems.

Today I stared at you from across the theater as usual but it felt different after our morning even though I know nothing has changed.

Today I contemplated pursuing a friendship with you but I'll always be too shy to speak to you and you were probably just being nice today, you probably think I'm really annoying.

Today I giggled at your antics before I realized that anyone who noticed would figure out I was staring and then my crush would be obvious and might reach your ears.

Today I heard you sing for the first time and it was pretty fantastic but I guess I was already expecting that based on how you sound whenever you speak.

Today I was struck by just how beautiful a man you are and I pondered it for hours but I still have no answer as to what makes you such a living work of art.

Today I closed my eyes for a really long time and all I could see, all I could imagine, was just me in your arms with my lips brushing against your neck.

Today I watched you applaud and I thought your hands were just so perfect and I really am weird for being so obsessed with hands.

Today I decided it was a good thing that soon I will never have to see you again because I know that if I had more time with you, I would most likely fall hopelessly in love with you.

Matthew Donovan

He was Matthew Donovan and he was pure and he could do no wrong. He was his calm and peaceful words and his desire to serve. He was the man who grew out of boyish desires and the man looked up to by all. But he was also Annelise Gabriel's blonde curls and electric blue eyes and her tiny waist small, shoulders, and he was the curves he could never look for. He was the vulgar thoughts that he knew were wrong and the base wants he had failed to guard himself against. He was falling but he had to get this out some way and he was at least not dragging her down with him while he became a worse man, the one he was not meant to be. He was Matthew Donovan and he was slave to the unknowing Annelise Gabriel.

SMS

Tried to abandon me

Leave me for dead but

I think I love you and

I couldn't bear the thought

Of losing you right now

If I lost you I would

Be lost and dead

You are my last good thing

You are my something to look forward t

And you might even be

My "special someone"

My "soul mate"

My "One"

So please don't leave me here

With nothing and no one

To hold me

Playing Favorites

After weeks and weeks

Of agonizing over you

Trying to recover from

My almost-loss of you

You began to be there

In all the ways I needed you

And I could finally tell you

Of my love and you wouldn't

Leave me again; everything

Fell correctly into place

But I know that nothing

Can ever stay perfect for long

So I wonder and I fear

What will happen when you

Change your mind again

And I fall out of

Your favor

Elude

I miss you every time

When I don't see you

I miss you more than I can bear

Going mad thinking of you

Longing to see you again

But you still manage

To escape my glance

To elude my grasp

And my longing thoughts

Are the closest I can get

To being by your side

Have You Again

Your life goes on without me

Was I really so easy to erase?

You're perfectly content without me

You don't miss me a bit

Meanwhile, I desperately miss you

Miss you so much I can't stand it

What I wouldn't give for one last chance

What I wouldn't trade

To have you again

Can't Keep Away

The thought of you makes me sick

I shake and I dread and I avoid

But I don't want to avoid

It's horrible for me to think it

But I can't just stop abruptly

I can't stop wanting to see you

I can't stop wanting you

And no matter how much I know

That I really need to keep away

I still risk it and look for you

I guess it's because I'm weaker

Weaker than my impulsive heart

My common sense says never

But my heart says pursue

God dammit, I love you still

And I just can't keep away

Multi-Hit Wonder

"So, like, you wanna come over later?"

I shake my head. "Nah, I have…stuff I need to do tonight." I don't elaborate and Genevieve doesn't ask. She's used to me being vague and she's never been too pushy.

"Alright," she says. "Hey, I got a lot of new things at the trunk show last week that I really wanted to show you, so you'll have to remind me next time you come over. It's a shame you couldn't have gone to it with me."

Of course I couldn't. Todd came back. I don't say this, but, rather nod and let the topic drop. I really had wanted to go, but I can never say no to Todd; I never could.

~X~

When I get home that night, he's waiting for me in dead silence. It looks like he hasn't been doing anything but I know better. He knew I was coming home and stopped whatever it was he had been doing, most likely. I give him a smile and he almost returns it before catching himself and turns it into a smirk.

"Good evening, my little pet," he says and I fight back a stupid grin.

"Good evening," I murmur. I go to sit beside him, hoping for a kiss, but today I am not that lucky, it seems. I feel like it might rain later.

"What time did you come over?" I ask.

"About two hours ago. I wanted to wait while you were with Genevieve. You didn't tell her anything, did you?"

"You know I wouldn't. Though Genevieve wouldn't voice any issue."

"Doesn't matter. It's not just about your friends hating me. I just never want to have my name tied to yours ever again."

His words don't throw me off that much. At this point, I've mostly outgrown the pang I feel whenever I'm reminded that he truly doesn't give a shit about me. I'm used to the fact that I am no longer a human being, I am his object.

"Yes, Todd."

"You're not allowed to say my name today."

I nod silently, unsure of what I should call him now. He would always get angry whenever I called him master; I wonder how he will react to lord. I make a note to try it later tonight if the chance arises.

"You know you're lucky I decided to take you back," he says. This is at least the fifteenth time in the past week that he's told me this and once again he makes it sound like he dumped me and I came crawling back, rather than the other way around. I try my best to be a good girl, so I don't mention that fact. It makes me want to strangle him.

He puts a heavy arm around me and he's, as always, surprisingly warm. You'd think I'd be used to it, but I always forget his cold attitude towards me is not reflected in his body temperature.

~X~

After watching a movie that he said he wanted me to know about, we sit in silence as he texts Katie. I don't know why he puts up with her abuse and cheating, and I think he should stop taking her back and just stay with me because I clearly adore him.

Tonight he's standing up for himself, telling her to hit the road, that he's done, but I know, she knows, and I think even he knows that she will come back soon and he will go running back and I will become a side attraction for whenever she's busy until I decide I won't put up with that. Then he will have a problem with Katie and I will take him back full time.

He sighs and his angry expression fades into a dejected frown as he puts his phone away. It is done.

"Why can't I find a woman who actually means it when she says that she loves me?"

"I mean it. I love you with all my heart, unconditionally. You know that," I say as he lays his head in my lap and I tangle my fingers in his thick hair.

"Oh, of course," he says, almost mockingly, but that is watered down by his depressed tone. "You're so hopelessly infatuated with me that I can do whatever I want with you. You're certainly convenient, but you hardly count as a comfort."

"I still love you," I say. I was expecting a response like that. It does not catch me off guard.

"As if you could ever stop," he says, and almost snickers before he remembers that he is supposed to be depressed right now.

I really wish he would cheer up or at least get really angry because I'm quite aroused and I can't ask for him to help with that. It has to be his suggestion.

It doesn't look like we will be having any of that fun tonight. He continues to sigh and make the occasional remark about how much he hates his life or how evil Katie is.

"Are you staying the night?" I ask, hoping maybe this might subconsciously give him the idea.

"No. You're going to have to drive me home." Todd doesn't have a car.

"How did you get here earlier?"

"Bus and a little bit of walking. Come on, take me back home, slut."

~X~

I drive Todd in silence, during a downpour, listening to him bitch about Katie for the ten minutes it takes to get to his apartment complex. I want him to invite me in, but I don't dare ask, I never dare ask. It doesn't matter how much I want or need him; I live only to serve him and his needs.

He gets out and disappears inside without a word of goodbye. I watch him with the typical longing then drive home and masturbate until three in the morning.

~X~

I'm sitting in a coffee shop with Samuel, hardly awake because of my late night. I'd drink coffee to wake myself up, but I really hate coffee and instead sip at a strawberry pineapple smoothie.

"Did you listen to the CD I lent you?" he asks.

"No, sorry, I've been pretty busy…"

"Busy?" Samuel snorts. "Since when do you ever do anything?"

"I've just been busy," I say defensively. A bit too defensively. Samuel can tell something is up and soon his expression shows that he knows exactly what is going on but doesn't want to believe it.

"Please don't tell me you're talking to Todd again."

"He'd be really pissed off if he knew that you knew. He told me not to tell anyone."

"God fucking dammit, Maddie! When are you going to learn your goddamn lesson?"

"Please don't do this right now…" I mumble, unable to bring myself to defend a choice that doesn't really deserve any defense.

"It pisses me the fuck off that you just keep taking that guy back. He's been abusing you and taking advantage of you since we were in high school. Just get rid of him already!"

"You don't understand, Samuel. I love him, alright? It's not something I can just stop because you told me to."

"Oh my god," he says with a groan. "It doesn't matter! You need to learn to love yourself. He treats you terribly and no one and nothing is worth the hell he puts you through."

We argue like this for a while before he gives one final frustrated groan and changes the subject. I text Todd under the table the whole time and I'm unsure if Samuel knows but I think he does.

~X~

The fatass invites himself over for dinner and I have to pick him up and swing through a Wendy's drive-thru on the way back. Both of us prefer fast food and he would probably find something to mock about my cooking anyway. I'm surprised by how little he always eats and wonder where his weight came from. I pretend I don't think he is fat to try and keep him happy.

He puts another movie on but gets distracted halfway through because he's laughing half to death over a story he wants to tell me.

"So, then, you know what Devin said to that? He-"

I pay as best attention as I can, but I frequently get distracted by his perfect complexion and full lips. As always, I want him, but he continues telling me stories for a full twenty minutes.

Finally, finally, his tone and focus shift and he is only telling his story half-heartedly now. His eyes are directed at where I sit, wanting a clear view of my ass, and there is a very noticeable bulge in his dark jeans.

"Maddie," he says. Oh, I do love when he says my name.

"Yes, my lord?"

He chuckles at this. "I like that. Anyway, I'm horny so you should probably get undressed and bend over…"

Excited, I do as I'm told, but it doesn't last long and I do not come. I am disappointed because I know he will do nothing more to pleasure me; however, I know he will allow me to pleasure myself, so long as he can watch.

~X~

When Todd sleeps beside me, I am usually overcome by one or two thoughts. Either how much I wish he would get hit by a train or how truly beautiful he is. Then the nightmares start, with the thrashing and clawing at his arms until he sometimes draws blood (this is why he always wears long-sleeved shirts). But I've learned that waking him up and trying to comfort him will never make them go away and I have ceased to give a fuck, so I only watch his nightly struggle for a little while before I get bored and fall asleep.

~X~

Sometimes when I see Henry I wonder why he hasn't tried to reunite with Selene because it's obvious that he still loves her. They only broke up because of they thought their lives were going to "go in different directions", but so far it seems like things would have worked out just fine and I had really hoped they wouldn't go through with it.

"But how have things been for you?" he asks.

"Same old," I lie. Or maybe it isn't a lie. As Samuel pointed out, Todd and I have been on and off since I was in the tenth grade.

"I feel that," he says, and we fall into silence. We never did much talking unless Selene was around. I always considered him my first sincere friend.

We sit in that silence for a while. Once, we could have found a topic to fill it even without Selene, but not anymore.

"You know," he says out of nowhere, "it's really not worth it."

"What are you talking about?"

"You know. And it's really not. Keep your sanity, your humanity…someone could use that in lyrics! Wait, no, that sounds fucking stupid."

"Henry, what the hell are you talking about?"

"You know. And I mean it. You're going to lose yourself a little more every day. It isn't worth it."

"What. Are. You. Talking. About?"

"You know."

"No, I don't."

"You know."

"I don't know."

"You know."

I do know, I'm just not sure how he knows.

~X~

I don't hear from Todd for two weeks, but I stop being worried after three days. After all, he loves pulling disappearing acts, and it's probably Katie. Once she comes back, he always drops me, and soon things will get rocky and he'll pick me back up, just to be safe. I don't know how he could keep taking someone like her back. It's honestly pathetic.

Anyway, I start talking to Michael again, and even though I'm mostly disinterested, he's too wrapped up in himself to notice. He and I only dated once, but it seems he always resurfaces whenever things with Todd turn sour.

"How are things with what's-his-name?" he asks, even though he very much knows Todd's name, considering he's Facebook stalked him several times in order to make hateful and borderline racist comments whenever he's brought up in conversation.

"Same as always," I respond, because, as I've come to realize, nothing ever changes. Everything follows a specific pattern and I'm not sure why, but I almost find that comforting.

"You kind of deserve that. But, forget about that, I..." I don't pay attention to what he says at that point, because I honestly don't care. I could care less about Michael, and actually find him to be rather disgusting, always have. Even when we were dating, I couldn't stand to look at him because I found him that repulsive then, too.

He tries to get me to suck him off, but because I've let myself remember how downright gross he is, I refuse. We bicker about it for a while, he calls me a bitch and "reminds" me of how he never even liked me and just dated me for convenience (the way I remember it, he was "completely heartbroken" and "cried the night we ended it", his words, but he called me a bitch then, too). I try to hold my own and make him feel bad, but in the end, I go home feeling terrible, even though he's disgusting so I don't truly care about his opinion of me.

I do wish he would stop making remarks about the size of my breasts though.

~X~

Michael and I have a few more encounters like that throughout those two weeks, and around the time I happen to make a Facebook status that he comments on, Todd texts me one day to say he's coming over, and I promptly send a text to Michael, telling him to fuck off, he's a creep, never talk to me again. I'm tempted to tell him that I only ever hang out with him to make Todd jealous, and throughout the end of our original relationship, I was cheating on him, but I decide not to because I might need him again later.

When Todd gets to my place, he doesn't mention his disappearance, nor does he mention Michael, even though that's his reason for reappearing. Instead, he tells me that he's really done with Katie for good this time and I pretend to believe him.

"We should see a movie," he says out of nowhere.

We've never been anywhere together in public, and I forget myself and let my excitement show. "Really? What do you wanna see and when should we go?"

"Well, it probably won't happen because we'd have to go pretty far out of town and I don't know if it's worth the trip when I could go somewhere in town by myself, or just take Drake instead."

"We wouldn't have to go out of town to see a movie..."

"Maddie, you know I don't want my name tied to yours, I've said that before. If someone sees us together, it would make me look bad for lowering myself. You can be such a stupid bitch sometimes."

I don't know what possesses me to do what I do, because his behavior is not out of the ordinary. Perhaps it was having my hopes crushed or maybe it was just because I had a new outfit I'd wanted to wear out. Whatever the reason, I react entirely differently than what is expected of me and what fits within the cycle.

"You can cut the superior asshole act," I snap.

"Excuse me?"

"Quit acting like you're doing me some huge favor by hanging out with me or that I'd ruin your image or whatever. It's the opposite and you know it. For one, no one likes you. You have maybe two friends and they both talk shit about you behind your back. Not to mention, you're ugly as fuck," I say. He's too shocked to interrupt me, so I continue. "You've been doing this since we were in high school, which just shows you'll never grow up, and I don't know why I put up with it, when I'm so clearly out of your league. And I've been nothing but nice to you, go out of my way for you, and even *worship* you and you repay me by acting like I'm some big inconvenience even though obviously you're fucking obsessed with me or you wouldn't keep crawling back. You're nothing but a petty little bitch who doesn't even come close to deserving me."

He stares at me in silence and that doesn't surprise me. After all, I can't believe I just said all that either. Why would I let out all those years of frustration now? And why did it have to be the most cliché, gurl-power rant I could possibly have thought up? So not only have I completely thrown everything out of whack by breaking the pattern, but I also sounded like a complete idiot doing so. I catch a glimpse of myself in a mirror and, to add insult to injury, realize my necklace doesn't even match my earrings.

"You...you have two seconds to apologize for that," he finally says. I stare at him as I contemplate sticking to my guns, but I guess he literally meant two seconds because the next thing I know he's raising his hand and then he has slapped me.

Nothing makes sense.

In all the time we've been together, with every insult and command, every time he left and came crawling back, even the times I've dumped him and sent him packing, he has never hit me. He has verbally and psychologically abused me, he has made me feel completely worthless, he has robbed me of my entire identity, but Todd has never hit me.

He must realize this as well because he looks terrified as he slowly backs away, then turns and runs out my door. I'm not sure what to do and so I lay face down on the floor and do not move until I remember that I really should listen to that CD Samuel lent me. It's been almost a month, after all.

~X~

As a week passes, I wonder what would happen if I told everyone the truth about the red mark that had been on my face for a short time. I know most would sympathize and tell me I deserved better and that he's a scumbag. Genevieve would threaten to call the police, Samuel would say he told me so but then go kick Todd's ass, Henry would have a long talk with me about self-respect and a longer talk with him, and Michael would probably offer sex as some sort of consolation.

But, of course, I can't tell anyone because Todd wouldn't like that and I am his property. I cannot displease him. So I keep quiet about him even though the pattern was destroyed and it left me very confused. I did not want to do anything to make him unhappy.

~X~

My phone buzzes and I look down at the screen. My heart doesn't even jump anymore; it's to the point where I almost know ahead of time when this is going to happen. I click to open it and read the message.

"Katie's pissing me the fuck off, so I want you to come over tonight cos if we bang it'll piss her off even more. Be there at eight exactly. Don't keep me waiting."

He really should stop putting up with Katie's abuse, I think as I drive to Todd's apartment complex.

Supersession

I will not speak

I will not let loose

The secret longing

That should not be

Allowed to exist

But I can see the

Things that bring

Me where I should

Never, ever tread

But I want to

I want to more

Than I could ever

Say; I want to

Play your game

On the ladder

And I do not

Care if I should

Fall off because

This is what I

Want to the point

It is a fixation, an

Obsession that

Has an all-consuming

Nature and I know

This will be my

Downfall and I

Can only hope

That it will be yours

As well

Will you change your name for me?

About the Author

Hannah Toney was born in Lexington, KY, on July 6th, 1996. She still resides there, as a student of psychology at the University of Kentucky. When she isn't writing, she spends her time making collages, watching cartoons (particularly *Jem and the Holograms* and *Bob's Burgers*), playing video games (*Dead Space* being her current favorite), reading (her list of favorite books is much too long to put here), collecting Monster High dolls and Harley Quinn merchandise, and hanging out with her boyfriend and best friend, Daniel Simpson. She's hoping to put out a few more collections, and perhaps to finally finish a full-length novel, but she doubts that will ever happen.